HOW & WHY?

ANIMALS PREPARE FOR WINTER

Elaine Pascoe is the author of more than 20 acclaimed children's books on a wide range of subjects.
Dwight Kuhn's scientific expertise and artful eye work together with the camera to capture the awesome wonder of the natural world.

Please visit our web site at: www.garethstevens.com
For a free color catalog describing Gareth Stevens Publishing's list of high-quality books
and multimedia programs, call 1-800-542-2595 or fax your request to (414) 332-3567.

Library of Congress Cataloging-in-Publication Data

Pascoe, Elaine.
  Animals prepare for winter / by Elaine Pascoe; photographs by Dwight Kuhn. — North American ed.
    p. cm. — (How & why: a springboards into science series)
  Includes bibliographical references and index.
  Summary: Describes some of the ways such different creatures as terns, chipmunks, bears, toads,
weasels, and praying mantises survive the winter.
    ISBN 0-8368-3006-7 (lib. bdg.)
    1. Animals—Wintering—Juvenile literature. [1. Animals—Wintering.] I. Kuhn, Dwight, ill. II. Title.
  QL753.P37   2002
  591.4'3—dc21   2001049484

This North American edition first published in 2002 by
Gareth Stevens Publishing
A World Almanac Education Group Company
330 West Olive Street, Suite 100
Milwaukee, WI 53212 USA

First published in the United States in 2000 by Creative Teaching Press, Inc., P.O. Box 2723, Huntington Beach, CA 92647-0723.
Text © 2000 by Elaine Pascoe; photographs © 2000 by Dwight Kuhn. Additional end matter © 2002 by Gareth Stevens, Inc.

Gareth Stevens editor: Mary Dykstra
Gareth Stevens designer: Tammy Gruenewald

Printed in the United States of America

1 2 3 4 5 6 7 8 9 06 05 04 03 02

HOW & WHY?

ANIMALS PREPARE FOR WINTER

by Elaine Pascoe
photographs by Dwight Kuhn

A SPRINGBOARDS INTO
SCIENCE
SERIES

Gareth Stevens Publishing
A WORLD ALMANAC EDUCATION GROUP COMPANY

Summer is over, and these gulls are flying south. Winter will bring cold, ice, and snow to the north, and food will be hard to find. The gulls will have more to eat in the warm south.

Many birds fly to warmer places for the winter season, but no bird migrates farther than the Arctic tern. This bird travels from the Arctic, near the North Pole, to the Antarctic, near the South Pole — a journey of 11,000 miles (17,700 kilometers)!

Animals that cannot fly south gather food before winter arrives. In fall, gray squirrels scurry around, searching for seeds and nuts. They bury some of what they find so they will have enough food for winter.

A chipmunk stores nuts in its underground den. The chipmunk hibernates, or sleeps through most of the cold weather, but it wakes up now and then to snack on the food it has stored.

Many other animals stay in their dens and hibernate during winter. A black bear looks for a cave or a burrow for its long winter nap.

A beaver family stays safe and warm through winter in a lodge in the middle of a frozen pond. Beavers eat branches they have stored underwater, beneath the ice.

A toad wiggles deep into decaying brush on the forest floor. A spotted salamander makes a winter home under fallen leaves.

Both of these animals hibernate in winter. When warm weather returns, the animals wake up.

Mice make warm winter nests beneath tree stumps and in barns and houses. They come out at night to look for food.

Mice must be very careful. Owls look for food at night, too — and they eat mice!

A weasel is one of many kinds of animals that grow new fur for winter. In summer, a weasel's fur is brown. In winter, it is white. The white fur blends in with the snow, so the weasel is hard to see when it is out searching for food.

A weasel might sneak through the snow to a farmer's chicken coop to find eggs.

Some animals cannot live through winter. A praying mantis, for example, cannot survive the cold. The eggs this insect lays in fall, however, are protected by a foamy egg case.

In spring, hundreds of babies hatch from the eggs. They grow during summer and lay their own eggs the following fall.

Can you answer these "HOW & WHY" questions?

1. Why do many birds fly south for winter?

2. Why are gray squirrels so busy just before winter arrives?

3. How do black bears spend the winter?

4. Why do mice have to be careful when they leave their winter nests?

5. How does its white winter fur help a weasel?

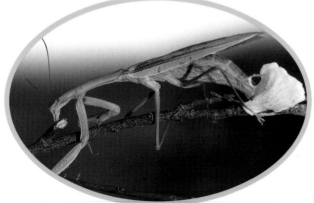

6. How does a praying mantis protect her eggs?

(See page 20 for answers.)

ANSWERS

1. Many birds fly south for winter because the south is warmer than the north in winter, and more food can be found in the south than in the icy, snow-covered north.

2. In fall, gray squirrels are busy gathering and burying seeds and nuts so they will have enough to eat in winter.

3. Black bears stay in caves or dens and hibernate for most of the winter.

4. When mice leave their nests to look for food at night, they might become food themselves — for hungry owls.

5. A weasel's white winter fur blends in with the snow, so the weasel cannot easily be seen as it searches for food.

6. The eggs of a praying mantis have a foamy egg case around them for protection.

The Beat Goes On

When animals hibernate, their breathing and heart rate slow down. Learn about your own heart rate by asking an adult to help you count how many times your heart beats in a minute when you are resting. Then run around or do some jumping jacks and count your heartbeats again. Compare how fast your heart was beating when you were resting and after you exercised. Try to find out how your counts compare to the heart rates of hibernating animals.

Chills Out!

Make a draft-stopper to help prepare your home for colder weather. Cut one leg off of an old pair of tights, stuff it with rags or cotton filling, and sew the end closed. You can decorate your draft-stopper with felt or other kinds of trimmings to make it look like a snake. Lay your draft-stopper on the floor along the bottom of an outside door to keep chilly air out of the house.

Butter Me Up!

Make a pinecone feeder for hungry birds that stay in your area all winter. Cover a pinecone with peanut butter. Be sure to get the peanut butter between the pinecone's scales. Then roll the pinecone in birdseed until it is completely covered. To make a hanger, tie heavy string to the top of the pinecone or have an adult help you attach some wire. Hang your homemade bird feeder outdoors and watch for wintertime visitors that come to get "buttered up!"

GLOSSARY

Antarctic: the region of cold, ice-covered land that surrounds the South Pole.

blends: mixes in completely.

brush (n): small trees and shrubs.

burrow: a hole or tunnel in the ground that an animal uses as its home.

coop (n): a cage or a pen for chickens or other poultry raised on a farm.

decaying: slowly rotting or decomposing.

den: a cave or some other sheltered place in the wild that an animal uses as its home.

egg case: a protective covering that surrounds the eggs of some animals.

foamy: full of foam, or extremely tiny bubbles that cling together in a mass.

gulls: large ocean birds with long wings and webbed feet.

hatch: to come, or break, out of an egg.

hibernates: spends the winter in an inactive, sleeplike state.

lodge: the home a beaver builds in water out of mud, branches, and rocks.

migrate: to move from one area or climate to another when seasons change.

protected: kept safe from harm.

scurry: to move around quickly, sometimes in a confused way.

stumps: the short tree trunks left in the ground after trees fall or are cut down.

survive: stay alive.

More Books to Read

Animals in Winter. Henrietta Bancroft and Richard G. Van Gelder (HarperCollins)

Animals on the Move. Allan Fowler (Children's Press)

Time to Sleep. Denise Fleming (Henry Holt & Company)

What Do Animals Do in Winter?: How Animals Survive the Cold. Melvin and Gilda Berger (Chelsea House)

When Winter Comes. Nancy Van Laan (Atheneum)

Videos

Animal Antics: Autumn. (Just for Kids Home Video)

Animal Antics: Winter. (Just for Kids Home Video)

Tales from the Wild: Tasha the Polar Bear. (National Geographic)

Web Sites

www.enchantedlearning.com/coloring/Hibernate.shtml

www.expage.com/page/mrsgwinter

www.yakscorner.com/animal/hibernation/

Some web sites stay current longer than others. For additional web sites, use a good search engine to locate the following topics: *animals in winter, hibernation,* and *migration.*

INDEX